JAMES FRITZ

James Fritz's other plays include *Parliament Square* (winner of the Judges' Award at the Bruntwood Prize for Playwriting; Royal Exchange Theatre, Manchester/Bush Theatre, London); *Start Swimming* (Young Vic/Summerhall); *Ross & Rachel* (MOTOR at Assembly George Square, Edinburgh Festival Fringe/59E59 Theaters, New York); *Four Minutes Twelve Seconds* (runner-up of Soho Theatre's 2013 Verity Bargate Award, nominated for an Olivier Award; Hampstead Theatre Downstairs) and *Lines* (Rosemary Branch Theatre).

Other Titles in this Series

James Fritz

THE FALL

NICK HERN BOOKS

London

www.nickhernbooks.co.uk

A Nick Hern Book

The Fall first published in Great Britain as a paperback original in 2016 by Nick Hern Books Limited, The Glasshouse, 49a Goldhawk Road, London W12 8QP

Reprinted in this revised edition in 2018

The Fall copyright © 2016, 2018 James Fritz

James Fritz has asserted his right to be identified as the author of this work

Cover photograph © Helen Maybanks

Designed and typeset by Nick Hern Books, London
Printed in Great Britain by Mimeo Ltd, Huntingdon, Cambridgeshire PE29 6XX

A CIP catalogue record for this book is available from the British Library

ISBN 978 1 84842 773 0

Woodland CARBON
www.woodlandcarbon.co.uk
NICK HERN BOOKS
Printed on Carbon Captured paper

The Fall was was commissioned by Paul Roseby in 2016 as part
of the National Youth Theatre's 60th anniversary and first
performed by the National Youth Theatre of Great Britain at the
Finborough Theatre, London, on 9 August 2016. The cast was
as follows:

C	Simeon Blake-Hall
D	Ben Butler
BOY	Oliver Clayton
B	Matilda Doran-Cobham
A	Hannah Farnhill
ONE	James Morley
TWO/LIAISON	Katya Morrison
GIRL/E	LaTanya Peterkin

Director	Matt Harrison
Designer & Costume Designer	Chris Hone
Sound Designer	Jak Poore
Lighting Designer	Seth Rook Williams

The Fall was revived by the National Youth Theatre of Great Britain at Southwark Playhouse, London, on 28 April 2018. The cast was as follows:

Josie Charles
Joshua Williams
Lucy Havard
Madeline Charlemagne
Troy Richards
Sophie Couch
Jesse Bateson
Jamie Ankrah
Niyi Akin
Jamie Foulkes

Director	Matt Harrison
Designer	Christopher Hone
Assistant Director	Melissa Taylor
Lighting Designer	Christopher Nairne
Sound Designer	Jak Poore
Choreographer	Rebecca Hesketh-Smith
Company Stage Manager	Emma Collins
Deputy Stage Manager	Robyn Amber-Manners
Assistant Stage Manager	Joseph Pearson
Production Manager	Gareth Edwards
Costume Supervisor	Helena Bonner
Wardrobe Mistress	Jenny Anderton
LX Operator	Benji Godley

Acknowledgements

Matt Harrison and our wonderful cast.

Beth, Kay, Anna, Paul and everyone at NYT.

Kate Hewitt and Nathan, James, Joe, Max, Olivia, Daniel, Sofia, Dipo, Tori, Vita and Aaron.

Anna Girvan and Ann, Anne, Annie, Boma, David, Rob, Lucrecia, Maureen, Patricia, Penny and Safina. Thank you all for sharing.

And Mum – for giving me her expert advice on finance and pensions and then for going all method during rehearsals.

J.F.

Characters

BOY
GIRL
ONE
TWO
LIAISON
A
B
C
D
NURSE

Note on Text

This play was written to be performed by young people.

Where I've offered you a choice – i.e. of song – feel free to add the cast's own personalities/interests/experiences to the text.

In the second and third parts there is no set gender for any character. I've occasionally used gender-specific pronouns in this text for clarity, but they can be switched.

Nobody should ever 'play old'.

This text went to press before the end of rehearsals and so may differ slightly from the play as performed.

FIRST

12

GIRL   You fell.

BOY   I never.

GIRL   You fell.

BOY   He tripped me.

GIRL   You fell.

BOY   The next lane he cheated.

GIRL   You got tangled up in your own stupid feet.

BOY   I still finished third.

GIRL   Congratulations.
        Third no that's really impressive.

BOY   I tripped but bounced right back up and finished
        third. Have you any idea how fast that makes me?

GIRL   Slightly less fast than two other guys?

BOY   I just ran out of time. If I hadn't been tripped I'd
        have dominated that race.

GIRL   Like I did with mine you mean?

BOY   No one cares about 1500m. It's a granny's race.

GIRL   I'd like to see a granny do what I just did. I left
        those girls in the dust.
        Sprinting's so boring. There's no point. Just as
        you're getting into it boom it's all over and you're
        like what happened? Middle distance we got to be
        smart. Tactical.

BOY   And what was your tactic?

GIRL   Running faster than everyone else.

BOY   Right.

GIRL   You ought to try it some time.

BOY	If I hadn't been tripped
GIRL	Fell.
BOY	If I hadn't been tripped he'd never have beaten me.
GIRL	But he did beat you.
BOY	But what I'm saying is
GIRL	But he did.
BOY	But what I'm saying is
GIRL	But he did.
BOY	You're enjoying this.
GIRL	Little bit yeah.

They kiss.

BOY	Right. Where we gonna go?
GIRL	I don't know what you mean?
BOY	Can we go back to yours?
GIRL	My mum's in.
BOY	So we'll be quiet.
GIRL	So you said that last time. Your house?
BOY	My little brother's in my bedroom.
GIRL	Get him nicely to leave the room. Worked before.
BOY	Yeah I don't know about that.
GIRL	What d'you mean?
BOY	Well. Last time we did it in my bed he left the room. But. He didn't go much further. If you know what I mean.
GIRL	Oh god. He was listening at the door?
BOY	He's twelve. He's just started wanking. It's a very exciting time for him.
GIRL	Okay your house is out.

BOY	The park?
GIRL	No.
BOY	The library?
GIRL	No.
BOY	What about round the back of the –
GIRL	Don't even finish that sentence. Nothing romantic ever started with the words 'round the back of'. What about booking a nice hotel?
BOY	Oh yeah that's a great idea. Let me just pull the money out my arse. I'm just gonna say this. McDonald's got a clean toilet.
GIRL	I am not having sex with you in a McDonald's. Again.
BOY	You know what? Chris said I could come by his work anytime.
GIRL	Okay.
BOY	Might be perfect.
GIRL	Well where does he work?
BOY	The kennels.
GIRL	Oh my
BOY	They've got this vet's room at the back.
GIRL	What is wrong with you?
BOY	It's got a bed in it.
GIRL	If you think I'm having sex in a kennel
BOY	Not in *a* kennel, at *the* kennels. Yeah. You're right. Shit.

There must be somewhere.

Oi. Wait a sec.

What about that butler?

GIRL   What are you on about?

BOY   That butler.
          The old guy whose house you clean?

GIRL   Mr Butler?

BOY   Yeah!

GIRL   He's not a butler that's just his name.

BOY   Right.

GIRL   Were you dropped on your head as a baby?

BOY   But.

          Didn't you say you have the keys to his house?

GIRL   Oh.

BOY   Yeah.

GIRL   Oh.

BOY   Yeah.

GIRL   I dunno. I could get in trouble. Isn't that breaking
          and entering?

BOY   Not if you have the keys.

GIRL   I mean. He's very old.
          I wouldn't wanna scare him. It might finish him off.

          Although.

          I've just remembered. He's sposed to be away all
          week.

BOY   Shit!
          You see that it's a fucking sign.

GIRL   I dunno.

BOY	Come on…
	It'll be romantic.
GIRL	Let's do it.
	We've got to remember to wash the sheets though.
BOY	Race you there.
GIRL	Maybe not eh? Don't want you falling over.

Mr Butler's house.

HELLO? MR BUTLER?

ANYONE HERE?

BOY	Woah. Look at this place. Always wondered who lives in these buildings.
GIRL	He don't even live here half the time. This is like house number three or something.
BOY	What was he, like a banker?
GIRL	A lawyer.

Hang on. Watch this.

She claps. The lights turn off.

BOY   Oh shit!

She claps again. They turn back on.

GIRL   He needs them because it takes him too long to get to the light switch. Although sometimes he's too weak to do a loud enough clap so he just stands there clapping in the dark.

The BOY *claps. The lights go off.*

BOY   Ha!

He claps again. The lights come back on.

Ha!

GIRL   Having fun?

BOY   I could do that all day.

            Look at some of this stuff. How old is he?

GIRL   Ninety-two.

BOY   Why's it smell like that?

GIRL   Like what?

BOY   It's got that old-man smell.

GIRL   I can't smell anything.

BOY   It stinks man. I need to open a window.

            So you come round and clean this place?

GIRL   Clean. Water the plants. Chat to him.

BOY   Why?

GIRL   Because I'm a nice person.
            And he pays me.

BOY   What's he like?

GIRL   He doesn't say much. Doesn't seem very happy.

BOY   Bet he loves you.

GIRL   He does actually.

BOY   Bet he hasn't seen a body like yours up close
            in years.
            'Nurse! Nurse! Time for my sponge bath.'

GIRL   You're disgusting.

BOY   He's disgusting. Dirty old perve.

GIRL   You got to be careful what you touch. If anyone
            finds out we were here I'll

            What the fuck are you doing?

BOY   What does it look like?

GIRL   It looks like you're doing press-ups.

BOY   Gotta stay in shape. Got a big race coming up.
              County trials.

GIRL   You got to do them now?

BOY   Every. Little. Helps.

GIRL   You're ridiculous.

              How many can you do?

BOY   How many d'you think?

GIRL   Fifty.

BOY   Easy.

GIRL   A hundred?

BOY   Won't even sweat.

GIRL   Go on then.

BOY   Right now?

GIRL   I've got time.

BOY   Okay.

              Press-ups. As many as he can do to exhaustion.

GIRL   That wasn't a hundred.

BOY   I did some before.

              Want a drink?

GIRL   Put that down.

BOY   Why?

GIRL   We can't steal from him.

BOY   Why not?

GIRL   Because it's wrong.

BOY   Look at this place. You think he's gonna mind?
              People like him have had it so easy. Imagine

living somewhere like this and it being no big
deal. I'm having a drink.

GIRL   Put it down. Please. I don't want to get into trouble.

BOY *starts to sing to her.*

His favourite song.

What are you

It's excruciating.

Stop it.

*Keeps singing verse after verse after verse.
Finally finishes.*

She starts to sarcastically slow clap him.

The lights flash on and off.

That was really
Something.

BOY   I know.
Come here.

GIRL   No.

BOY   Have a drink.

GIRL   Just one.

A small one.

BOY   This his picture?

GIRL   Yeah.

BOY   Look at his eyes. He looks like a skeleton.
Imagine being that old.

GIRL   Will you still fancy me when I look like that? When
my skin's all wrinkled and my body's all saggy?

BOY   Aw, baby. Of course not.

GIRL   Oh my god.

BOY	Just being honest.
	If my body ever looks like that I'm just gonna end it there and then. Bullet to the head. BAM.
GIRL	Do you ever wonder? Nah. Never mind.
BOY	What?
GIRL	You remember last Friday when we, you know. Did what we did.
BOY	Do I remember? It's on constant replay up here.
GIRL	Sometimes I think after we've done something that
BOY	Intimate? GIRL Dirty.
GIRL	Right. When we've done something like that it's not long until the thought pops into my head
BOY	What?
GIRL	Seriously actually never mind you're gonna think it's weird.
BOY	You gotta tell me now.
GIRL	Well I sometimes can't help but think that whatever sex thing we've just done has almost certainly been done by my grandparents as well.
BOY	Oh my god.
GIRL	I know.
BOY	That's what you think after we
GIRL	Well not every time. Just sometimes.
BOY	You're sick.
GIRL	Not during. Never during. Just after. Sometimes. It's just interesting isn't it?
BOY	No!

GIRL	It is. It's interesting. Nobody ever thinks of their grandparents doing
BOY	There's a reason.
GIRL	Having
BOY	There's a reason. You're disgusting. That's disgusting.
GIRL	It's just a thought.
BOY	Shit.
GIRL	What?
BOY	Well now I'm thinking about my grandparents doing it.
GIRL	See!
BOY	Oh man I can't stop picturing it.
GIRL	Stop picturing your grandparents doing what we did last Friday.
BOY	Gah.
GIRL	Stop thinking about your grandparents doing every dirty thing we've ever done.
BOY	Stop.

The BOY *retches.*

GIRL	And quite a lot we haven't done.

The BOY *retches.*

Their wrinkly skin rubbing up against

He retches again and again.

BOY	I said stop!
GIRL	Oh my god. Are you actually retching?
BOY	ENOUGH.
GIRL	Alright. I'm only playing. Wait. You're not actually annoyed are you?

BOY   No.
            I'm just. Why d'you gotta spoil the mood like that?
            Things were all sexy and now it's ruined. Fuck's
            sake.

GIRL   Jesus I'm sorry.

BOY   It's disgusting it's fucking disgusting.

GIRL   Where are you going?

BOY   The bathroom. I need a piss.
            Is that alright?

GIRL   Jesus.

            BOY *leaves. Comes back.*

            Yes?

BOY   I don't know where the bathroom is.

GIRL   Down the hall.

            He leaves again.

            GIRL *does something young and impressive.*

BOY   I'm sorry. About before.

GIRL   Hmm.

BOY   I overreacted.

GIRL   You think?

BOY   It's just. I can't handle that stuff. It makes me feel
            sick. Like I have an allergic reaction or something.

            It's a thing I have. I just. Don't like thinking.
            Old people man. They're fucking disgusting.
            I'm sorry. I'm over it now.

            He's got a lot of pills.
            What's wrong with him?

GIRL   Lots of things.

BOY   It's shit like this keeping us alive too long.

GIRL   What about your nan?

BOY   What about my nan?

GIRL   Well your nan's the same age would you say that
        about her?

BOY   That's different.

GIRL   Why?

BOY   Because my nan's not some old man. She's young
        at heart.
        You know she's old in years but in her mind she's
        sharp. She does the Sudoku.

        You know what, we came here to have sex I dunno
        why we're talking about my nan.

GIRL   You started it.

BOY   Come here. Let's just have a nice time.

        They kiss.

GIRL   I saw that.

BOY   What?

GIRL   You were looking in the mirror while we kissed.

BOY   Was I?
        Just making sure everything's in order.

GIRL   You're incredible.

BOY   I know.

        They kiss again.

        Where's the bedroom?

GIRL   In here.

BOY   It's dark.

GIRL   Turn the lights on.

        He claps. Nothing. He claps again. Nothing.

        There isn't a clapper in here.

BOY	Where's the light switch? I can't find the button.
GIRL	That bodes well.
BOY	Here we go.

The lights come on.

Okay. I am gonna

GIRL	What are you gonna?
BOY	I am gonna FUCK. A FOOT.
GIRL	What?
BOY	A foot.
GIRL	A foot?
BOY	A foot

There!

GIRL	What are you oh shit Mr Butler I'm so sorry! We didn't know you were here.

A beat.

MR BUTLER?

BOY	Why's he naked?
GIRL	I dunno.
BOY	My eyes!
GIRL	MR BUTLER?
BOY	He's not moving. Is he dead?
GIRL	MR BUTLER HELLO HELLO CAN YOU HEAR ME IT'S ME THE GIRL WHO WATERS YOUR PLANTS.
BOY	Never seen a dead body before.
GIRL	MR BUTLER.

BOY   Look at his skin.
All shrivelled and

GIRL   We should probably call someone.

BOY   What are those black marks. Skin flaps. His stomach.

BOY *retches*.

GIRL   Are you retching again?

BOY   No I. Just give me a minute.
What are you doing?

GIRL   Checking his pulse.

BOY   Don't touch him!

GIRL   I can't feel anything.

BOY   Touching dead old-man skin.

GIRL   Look at this. It's empty.

BOY   So?

GIRL   So maybe he took them all?

BOY   Or maybe he took the last one this morning.

GIRL   What should we do?

BOY   You should stop touching him is what we should do.

GIRL   We should call the doctor.

BOY   Don't think that'll do him much good.

GIRL   The police then.

BOY   Dickhead. We're not sposed to be here.

GIRL   Don't call me a dickhead you're a dickhead

BOY   Least I don't go around touching old dead men.

GIRL   We can't just leave him.

BOY   Why not he's not gonna mind. EXCUSE ME DO YOU MIND IF WE LEAVE YOU HERE?
See he doesn't mind.

GIRL   How would you like it?

BOY   I'd be dead.

GIRL   What if it was your dead nan then?

BOY   Why you talking bout my nan again?

GIRL   I'm just saying

BOY   My nan's not dead don't say my nan's dead.

GIRL   But if she was.

BOY   She's young at heart!

GIRL   We should at least cover him up.
            Get a sheet.

BOY   From where?

GIRL   Er. The bed?

BOY   Why?

GIRL   Because it's dignified. We can't leave him here all
            naked and alone.

BOY   Wait.
            He moved.

GIRL   No he didn't

BOY   Wait. He did his finger it moved.
            Oh shit it did it again.

GIRL   MR BUTLER?

BOY   Don't talk to it!
            You said there was no pulse.

GIRL   There wasn't.

BOY   He's definitely moving.

GIRL   Help me get him on the bed.

BOY   Really?

GIRL   What's the matter?

BOY   Ain't you got some gloves or

         Fine. Okay. Deep breath.

GIRL   You alright?

BOY   Yep.

GIRL   You're not gonna be sick?

BOY   Nope.

GIRL   One. Two. Three. Up.

BOY   He's so light.

GIRL   IS THAT BETTER MR BUTLER?

BOY   How can he be that light?

GIRL   ARE YOU COMFORTABLE?

BOY   His mouth. His eyes.

         What should we do?
         Call an ambulance? Right? That's what we
         should do.

GIRL   You think so?

BOY   Of course. That's what people do.

         Okay. MR BUTLER WE'RE GONNA CALL
         YOU AN AMBULANCE.
         DID YOU UNDERSTAND MR BUTLER?
         HANG ON YEAH.

         Okay.

         It's ringing.

         The GIRL *snatches his phone. Hangs up.*

         What are you doing?

GIRL   I. Dunno.

BOY   Give me my phone back.

GIRL   I

            No

BOY   This isn't funny.

GIRL   It's not sposed to be.
            I'm just thinking

BOY   He's dying he's

GIRL   Maybe. Maybe.

            Maybe we shouldn't.

BOY   What?

GIRL   Maybe we shouldn't call the ambulance.

            We weren't sposed to be here today.

BOY   Stop messing about.

GIRL   And if we weren't supposed to be here today we
            weren't sposed to find him like this.

BOY   You worried about getting into trouble?

GIRL   No.

BOY   He's dying.

GIRL   I'm saying what if this is what's sposed to happen.

            What if he's ready to go? We shouldn't intervene.

            MR BUTLER?

BOY   He can't hear you!

GIRL   Maybe he doesn't even want us to. MR BUTLER
            DO YOU WANT US TO CALL AN
            AMBULANCE?

BOY   You're scaring me gimme the phone.

GIRL   I don't think I should. He's ninety-two.

BOY   That don't make a difference.

GIRL	Imagine being him. Every day you wake up. You're tired. Your body doesn't work properly. Looks like that. You said it. You'd kill yourself.
BOY	I was joking. We. We can't just let him die.
GIRL	Why not?
BOY	Because that's not what people do! Gimme the phone.
GIRL	No.
BOY	Gimme the fucking phone.
GIRL	IT'S ALRIGHT MR BUTLER I'M WITH YOU.
BOY	You're sick. You're twisted. His breathing. Oh my god listen to his breathing.
GIRL	It's okay.
BOY	I can't watch this I don't want to watch this Mr Butler don't die please don't die please don't die what do I do tell me what to do what do I do? I'm gonna find a phone there must be a house phone or something to call an ambulance or They can tell us what to do how to save him or
GIRL	It's alright.
BOY	No.
GIRL	It's alright.
BOY	He's gonna die.
GIRL	I know.
BOY	And you're just gonna watch?
GIRL	I'm gonna make him comfortable. I'll give you the phone. Call the ambulance if you want.

BOY   Okay.

GIRL   But he's not gonna thank you.

           I've been coming round here for weeks. He gets
           up. Sits in his chair. Eats. Goes to bed. That's
           his day.

           There's nothing for him to do. No one for him to
           talk to. When I ask him a question it's like I'm an
           alien. Maybe he's just tired.

           You can call the ambulance. See if they can keep
           him alive a bit longer. Tell yourself you did the
           right thing.

           Or you can help me make him comfortable.

BOY   I don't want to see someone die.

GIRL   I know you don't. I know.

           IT'S ALRIGHT MR BUTLER WE'RE HERE
           WITH YOU.

BOY   I'm not sure. Not sure I can stay here.

GIRL   IT'S OKAY MR BUTLER. SHHH. SHHH.

           You don't have to. You wait downstairs. I'll stay.
           I don't think it'll take long.

           IT'S OKAY.

           IT'S OKAY.

           IT'S OKAY.

           I'M HERE. I'M HERE WITH YOU.

           BOY goes to leave. Can't quite look away.

BOY   He's so small.

GIRL   Yeah.

           They watch Mr Butler for a while.

BOY   Do you really think it's that bad?

             Being that old?

GIRL   Maybe.

             I don't know.

             I spose we'll find out soon enough.

SECOND

ONE	Ready?
TWO	Yep.
ONE	Don't be nervous.
TWO	I'm not nervous.
ONE	She's just a woman.
TWO	She's your mum.
ONE	She won't bite.
TWO	What's she like?
ONE	She'll love you. Mum, this is
TWO	Nice to meet you Jean. Did she like me?
ONE	She didn't hate you. I love you? Your childhood room.
TWO	Embarrassing.
ONE	All these trophies.
TWO	1500m. They like to keep them.
ONE	First. Champion. First. Did you ever lose a race?
TWO	Oh
ONE	Oh baby yeah
TWO	Oh oh
ONE	Oh oh yeah oh Mum! Get out of here.
TWO	Your mum's seen me
ONE	Yeah.

TWO	She's seen my
ONE	She'll find it funny!
	Mum's got you a present.
TWO	Thank you it's... um.
ONE	I'm running late. Look after Mum will you?
TWO	Just the two of us?
ONE	I won't be long.
TWO	So. Er. Jean. How's... work?
ONE	Marry me?
TWO	Of course!
	I'm pregnant.
ONE	You what?
TWO	Yeah.
ONE	Oh my god.
TWO	Yeah.
ONE	Can we afford it?
TWO	Absolutely not.
ONE	I don't care. Do you care?
TWO	No!
ONE	Oh my god!
TWO	Hello little Liam.
	We are going to take such good care of you.
ONE	Mum, this is Liam.
TWO	Thanks for the advice Jean but this is really none of your business. Your mum.

ONE   I know.

TWO   Sometimes.

ONE   I know.

TWO   Thanks for watching him Jean.

ONE   Rent's going up.

TWO   We need more nappies.

ONE   Thanks for watching him Mum.

TWO   Happy anniversary!

ONE   I love you.

TWO   Putting the rent up.

ONE   Again?

TWO   He needs clothes.

ONE   Again?

TWO   Keeps growing.

ONE   We can't afford it.

TWO   The walls are damp.

ONE   Fucking toys everywhere.

TWO   No space.

ONE   First day at school!

TWO   So grown up.

ONE   There's a job at work.

TWO   You'll do great.

ONE   I didn't get it.

TWO   The damp's got worse.

ONE   I'll speak to the landlord.
           I spoke to the landlord.

TWO   And

ONE   He'll sort the damp.

TWO   Great.

ONE   But the rent's going up.

TWO   Shit.

ONE   That means

TWO   We can't afford

ONE   I'll start looking.

TWO   We can't move again.

ONE   We have to.
           You told her?

TWO   Of course.

ONE   Why?

TWO   She's your mum.

ONE   Can't believe

TWO   I asked for help.
           She wants to help. Do you have any idea how
           lucky you are?

ONE   It's her flat.

TWO   It's worth a lot.

ONE   It's her home.

TWO   She wants to sell it.

ONE   To give us money?

TWO   To help us out.

ONE   No.

TWO   We could start saving. Buy somewhere.

ONE   It's charity.

TWO   You're her son.

ONE	That doesn't mean
TWO	Liam's her grandson.
ONE	So she should just
TWO	The world
ONE	The world is fine.
TWO	What happens when we're old? How will he take care of us?
ONE	That's years away.
TWO	We've got no savings.
ONE	We'll manage.
TWO	No pension.
ONE	I'll get one.
TWO	We're still fucking renting.
ONE	So what? So's everyone.
TWO	You're nearly fifty.
ONE	I'm forty-eight.
TWO	She wants to do this.
ONE	No. I'm sorry.

When she dies

That flat is ours.
And we can sell it

Or live there even.
But not. Till. Then. I'm sorry. Can't do it to her.
She's my mum. It's her home.
Her and my dad worked hard to buy that place.

TWO	It was easier then.
ONE	We'll move a bit further out. Find somewhere cheaper. Who knows? Maybe we'll have a garden.

So. There's no garden.

We'll fix it up.

Liam. This is your new home.

TWO	School uniform.
ONE	How much?
TWO	Football boots.
ONE	His cough.
TWO	Getting worse. Council tax.
ONE	Another school trip.
TWO	Gas bill's late.
ONE	It's broken again.
TWO	Call the landlord.
ONE	Hi Mum.
TWO	How can it be this hard?
ONE	I know. I'm late for work.
TWO	Working late again.
ONE	TV licence.
TWO	Already? Credit card.
ONE	Overdue.
TWO	How much?
ONE	Rent's going up. Hi Mum.
TWO	Your mum.
ONE	She's fine.
TWO	Seems a bit funny.
ONE	What do you mean?
TWO	Her flat.

ONE   Always been messy.

TWO   Her hands.

ONE   What?

TWO   Bit shaky.

ONE   You're seeing things.

TWO   Jean. Can I help you with that?

ONE   It's

           It's Mum.

TWO   What?

ONE   Had a fall.

TWO   A fall. How bad?

ONE   She broke her hip. They can fix that, right?

TWO   Hi Jean.

ONE   Hi Mum how you doing?

TWO   She looks

ONE   Frail. It's just a hip. It'll get better.

TWO   At her age?

ONE   She's still a young woman.

TWO   She's really not.
           Can't walk.
           Wash herself. At least for a while.

ONE   They're saying
           Home care.

TWO   Okay.
           It's free right?

ONE   Of course. It must be.

           So. It's not free.

TWO   How much?

ONE   A lot.

TWO   What. Why?

ONE   Mum's too rich.

TWO   That's a joke.

ONE   I know.

TWO   She can barely afford

ONE   I know. But her savings.

TWO   She needs those.
           That doesn't seem

ONE   Fair?

TWO   Surely there's some way?

ONE   No.

TWO   A grant or

ONE   No one's told me anything.

TWO   So what?

ONE   Her savings. We stretch them.

TWO   And then?

ONE   I don't know. Fuck this

TWO   I know.

ONE   I'm not ready for this it's not fair.
           I'm not ready for this it's not fair.
           I'm not ready for this it's not fair.
           I'm not ready for this it's not fair.
           I'm not ready for this it's not fair.
           I'm not ready for this it's not fair.
           I'm not ready for this it's not fair.
           I'm not ready for this it's not fair.
           I'm not ready for this it's not fair.
           I'm not ready for this it's not fair.
           I'm not ready for this it's not fair.

I'm not ready for this it's not fair.
I'm not ready for this it's not fair.
I'm not ready for this it's not fair.
I'm not ready for this it's not fair.
I'm not ready for this it's not fair.
I'm not ready for this it's not fair.
I'm not ready for this it's not fair.
I'm not ready for this it's not fair.
I'm not ready for this it's not fair.

Mum this is Angela.

TWO   She'll be coming in to help.

ONE   Angela

TWO   Hi Jean, how you doing?

ONE   Hi Mum, what's up?

TWO   Hi Angela, how's she been?

ONE   You comfortable enough Mum?

TWO   Can I get you anything Jean?

ONE   Let me do that for you Mum.

TWO   Don't worry about it Jean.

ONE   I said let me do that Jesus Christ.

Sorry Mum I'm

ONE   Hi Angela.

TWO   Hi Angela.

ONE   Angela that's not good enough. That's not fucking good enough.

TWO   Angela's really upset.

ONE   So she should be.

TWO   You screamed at her.

ONE   Fifteen minutes she spends with Mum.

TWO   It's all she's allowed.

ONE   It's not enough. The amount it's costing.

TWO   It's not her fault.
             The company.
             Say sorry.

ONE   Why should I?

             Angela. I'm really sorry.

             I thought she'd be better by now.

             I could stop work.

TWO   No.

ONE   Take care of her.

TWO   We can't afford that.

ONE   What choice do we have?

TWO   We need your income.

ONE   She's my mum. I have to. We'll cut back on

TWO   Food? Electricity?

ONE   Make it work. Somehow.
             It's not for ever.

TWO   What if she lives
             Ten years. Fifteen?

ONE   Breakfast Mum?

TWO   Liam! Time for school.

ONE   Lunch Mum?

TWO   No Liam love we can't afford that. I'm sorry.

ONE   Don't worry Mum it's alright.

TWO   What time is it?

ONE   3 a.m.

TWO   She's calling again?

ONE   I've got to go she's frightened.

TWO	Go back to bed Liam it's alright.
ONE	Just going to see your nana.
TWO	How can it be like this?
ONE	Don't know.
TWO	How can there be no help?
ONE	There's something I should
TWO	You quit your job?
ONE	I'm sorry.
TWO	When?
ONE	I'm sorry.
TWO	Why didn't you tell me?
ONE	I couldn't.
TWO	Where have you been going?
ONE	Mum's.
TWO	But your paycheck. How have we been
ONE	A loan. I took a loan.
	But I didn't realise the interest was
TWO	Oh Jesus.
ONE	I'm so sorry.
TWO	What are we going to do?
	Eviction notice.
ONE	What does that mean?
TWO	What do you think?
ONE	Where will we go?
TWO	Your mum's. We'll have to move in.
ONE	We won't all fit.

TWO	We'll have to. She can keep her bedroom and we'll go in the living room.
ONE	All of us?
	I'll talk to her.
TWO	You promise?
ONE	I'll talk to her.
	Mum. You alright in there?
	Mum? Mum??
	It's my mum. She fell again. In the shower. Come quick.
TWO	How is she?
ONE	You know her. 'Don't worry about me. I'm not finished yet.'
TWO	So.
ONE	So.
TWO	What now? A home?
ONE	Residential care. The cost
TWO	Per month?
ONE	Per week.
TWO	Fuck off.
ONE	I know.
TWO	How is that possible?
ONE	Don't know.
TWO	How does she
ONE	The flat. She sells it.

TWO   No.

ONE   That's the law.

TWO   But we

ONE   I know. What else can we do?

          Off to Jobcentre.

TWO   Great.

ONE   Can you check in on Mum?

TWO   Course.

ONE   She's a bit agitated.

TWO   Good luck.

ONE   Make sure she rests.

TWO   Jean. Hi Jean. How you doing?

          It's me.

          Jean. Are you okay?

          Hi love.

ONE   Hi. What's up?

TWO   Where are you?

ONE   Jobcentre what's wrong?

TWO   Your mum she's
          She's gone.

ONE   Oh.

TWO   I found her
          In bed.

ONE   Right.

          Okay.

TWO   In her sleep. She went for a nap and. Didn't
          wake up.

ONE   Okay.
            Peaceful you think?

TWO   Yes peaceful.

ONE   That's good. That's good.
            Liam mate.
            Some bad news. Your nana.

TWO   How is he?

ONE   Cried a lot.

TWO   How are you?

ONE   I don't know.

            Relieved. I suppose.

            In a home. She would've hated it.

TWO   Yeah.

ONE   What do I do now? I don't know what to do.

TWO   It's alright. It's alright.

ONE   Which song?

TWO   Why not both?

ONE   She was

TWO   Remember when she

ONE   How she always

TWO   That time

ONE   Oh my god I'd forgotten.

TWO   She could be. Sometimes.

ONE   Yeah.

TWO   If you caught her in the wrong mood.

ONE   Oh god yeah.

TWO   But then others.

ONE   She was

TWO   Still though.

ONE   She died at home that's

TWO   Her own bed.

ONE   That's good. She didn't want to lose
            This place.
            Maybe now we can get a place of our own.
            They wanted that. That'll help, won't it?

TWO   Yes. That'll help.
            Are you okay?

ONE   I love you.
            I love you so much.

TWO   Morning.

ONE   Hmm.

TWO   What's up?

ONE   The police.

TWO   Police?

ONE   They rang. Mum's body

TWO   What about it?

ONE   They're not releasing the body.

TWO   Why not?

ONE   Cause of death.

TWO   Cause of death?

ONE   They're trying to determine.

TWO   Oh. That's.

ONE   Odd right?
            Suffocation. Is what they think.

TWO   Her pillows?

ONE   Probably

TWO   An accident?

ONE   Probably.
            But there was a mark.

TWO   What mark?

ONE   A bruise. Under her nose.

TWO   Oh. That's odd.

ONE   Foul play. Maybe.

TWO   That's ridiculous.

ONE   I know.

TWO   Ridiculous.

ONE   Of course. Because you

TWO   I found her.

ONE   She went for a nap and you found her.

TWO   That's right.

ONE   You were there. You were the only one there.
            No one else.

TWO   What. What are you saying?

ONE   Nothing.

TWO   Because if you're

ONE   I'm not.

TWO   Implying or

ONE   No no. That's not

            But

            You didn't. Did you?

TWO   Oh my god.

ONE   Did you?

TWO   How can you

ONE   Please.

TWO   You ask me?

ONE   Look me in the eye.

TWO   I am.

ONE   Look me in the eye and tell me.

TWO   Maybe you should sit down.

ONE   Oh god.

TWO   It's not what you think so

ONE   You did it?

TWO   No listen.

ONE   You killed her?

TWO   No!

        Well.

        I helped.

ONE   Helped?

TWO   She asked me.

ONE   What.

TWO   She asked me. To help her.
        We were talking.
        She didn't want to
        Move
        And
        Since her fall
        The pain
        And
        Our situation
        Her flat
        Those sharks
        She knew
        That this was best
        So she asked me.

I'm sorry.
I love you.
For us.
For Liam.
Her flat.
It's meant for you.
Always.
That's what she said.
She asked me.
I'm tired she said.
I'm ready.
I said no
But
She kept asking
And.
I love you.

ONE   How

TWO   Pills.
And I put a pillow
Resting on her.
I love you.
She didn't fight.
It was gentle.
I promise.
She knew.
Every year in that home
Would've been
Worse for her.
Worse for us.
Worse for Liam.
Worse for Liam.
I love you.
So.
Since her fall.
So much pain
And
She said

Eskimos.

ONE   Eskimos?

TWO   When Eskimos get old they walk out into the
            snow and die.
            Choose their time.
            And I thought.
            If I was her.
            What would I want?

ONE   When. When did she ask you?

TWO   A week or so.

ONE   You knew? All that time?

TWO   Yes.

ONE   You lied.

TWO   Yes.

ONE   Why?

TWO   She didn't want.
            Knew you wouldn't.
            Understand.

ONE   She was right.

TWO   It was very brave.

ONE   Brave?

TWO   Yes.

ONE   Stupid.
            The police.
            Oh my god.

TWO   I know.

ONE   Oh my god.

TWO   What. What should we say?

ONE   We?
            I don't know.
            I need to get out of here.

TWO	Where?
ONE	I don't know.
TWO	She asked me. I love you. Please. She asked me. You're back.
ONE	Yep.
TWO	Where?
ONE	Hotel.
TWO	You hungry?
ONE	No.
TWO	The police. They're releasing the body.
ONE	Oh.
TWO	No foul play.
ONE	How?
TWO	I don't know. Luck I guess. That's that. We can have the funeral.
ONE	Did she really ask you?
TWO	Of course.
ONE	Because Maybe you're right. She's right. It's for the best. And I would never Could never have.
TWO	I know.
ONE	So. Maybe. It must have been hard.

TWO   It was.

ONE   But I can't
         One thing.
         'I'm not finished yet.'

TWO   What?

ONE   You remember she kept saying
         'I'm not finished yet'.
         I know Mum.
         Course you're not.
         'I'm not finished yet.
         I'll be here a long time yet.'

TWO   Something people say.

ONE   Maybe.

         But.

         Why would she?
         If she knew.

         If she'd already asked you.

TWO   This flat. Her flat. We've got nothing else.
         It's a life raft.

         I loved her.
         She was a good woman.
         Had a good life.
         But we couldn't afford.

         This had to happen.
         For Liam.
         You understand that don't you?

You can hate me if you want. For the rest of our
lives you can hate me.
But think about him. He's what's important.
Not us. Not your mum.

She asked me to do it.
I need you to believe that.
For all our sakes.
Do you believe that?

ONE   She asked you to do it.

THIRD

Years later.

Four people with enough space for two people.

B	Just arrived?
A	Yes. I'm
C	Hello!
B	That's you in there.
C	Petra turn off the TV.
A	They said I was in a two-person unit.
D	I was watching that.
B	This was a two-person unit. Now it's a four-person unit.
D	Don't you read the news?
A	I'm sorry?
D	How old are you then?
C	You can't ask that.
A	Eighty-four.
D	I'm eighty-five.
B	You're eighty-six we had your birthday last week.
D	I'm eighty-five fuck you.
B	Where have you come from?
D	Don't put that there! That's not your space. Over there over there is yours.
B	Don't worry he can be a bit

D	I'll be gone soon then you can do what you like.
C	Shared bathroom's over there.
B	Try not to spend hours in it like some people.
D	I need to spend time in there. I need to look good.
B	Food dispensed there.
D	Petra I'm thirsty.
B	Medicine there.
C	Petra painkillers please.
A	How is the food?
C	Quite nice.
B	Inedible.
D	Where I'm going there's a proper chef.
A	Where are you going?
D	I'm not staying long. My nephew's paying for me to move to a proper place.
A	That's nice.
D	It's not nice it's fucking lovely. It's fucking lovely.

A *finds something*.

B	That was Sammy's.
C	He was here before.
B	You can throw it away if you like.
A	Petra. I'm home.
LIAISON	HOW ARE YOU SETTLING IN?
A	Okay. I didn't realise I'd be sharing with
LIAISON	I SEE YOU WERE HOSPITALISED?

A   A few weeks back. I had a fall and
                It hurts still. But. Better.

LIAISON   I'M GLAD TO HEAR IT.

                NOW. YOU'RE AWARE OF WHAT WE'RE
                HERE TO DISCUSS?

A   Yes. And. I know I said I wanted to know more
                but I'm not sure

LIAISON   THAT'S ABSOLUTELY FINE. THE DECISION
                WILL ALWAYS BE ENTIRELY YOUR OWN.
                NO ONE IS HERE TO FORCE YOU INTO
                ANYTHING.

                WE UNDERSTAND WHAT A DIFFICULT
                CHOICE IT IS.

A   Does it. Does it hurt?

LIAISON   NO. IT'S COMPLETELY PAINLESS. THEY
                MAKE SURE THAT EVERYTHING IS VERY
                COMFORTABLE.

A   Right. And. The family compensation

LIAISON   HIGHER THAN IT'S EVER BEEN.
                THE FIGURES ARE ALL THERE IN FRONT
                OF YOU.
                NEXT OF KIN'S YOUR SON HAVE I GOT
                THAT RIGHT?

A   Yes. That's

LIAISON   IT COULD REALLY MAKE A DIFFERENCE
                TO HIM. DOES HE KNOW THAT YOU'RE
                CONSIDERING THIS OPTION?

A   No. Does that matter?

LIAISON   IF YOU'RE THINKING SERIOUSLY ABOUT
                THIS WE RECOMMEND TALKING IT
                THROUGH WITH THOSE CLOSE TO YOU. IT
                CAN OBVIOUSLY BE A VERY DIFFICULT
                THING FOR MANY FAMILIES TO ACCEPT.

ULTIMATELY THOUGH, IT'S YOUR
DECISION. THEY CAN'T STAND IN
YOUR WAY.

A   Are your parents still alive?

LIAISON   YES.

A   Do they live with you?

LIAISON   NO.

PERHAPS WE COULD MEET AGAIN. NEXT
TIME YOUR SON IS VISITING?

WE DON'T HAVE A CONTACT NUMBER FOR
HIM DO YOU HAVE ONE YOU CAN GIVE US?

A   No.

I. I'm not.

I'm going to think about it some more. If that's
alright.

LIAISON   OF COURSE. THAT'S FINE.

IF YOU LIKE I COULD GIVE YOU SOME
LITERATURE TO TAKE AWAY?

B   Petra what's the news today?

D   Petra I'm hungry.

C   Petra painkillers please.

D   Petra I'm still hungry.

B   Petra play [*favourite TV show*]

D   Petra turn it down.

B   Petra turn it up.

D   Petra turn it down.

B   Petra turn it up. Full volume.

C   Petra send a message to my kids.

A   Petra. What time is it?

B	Petra I'm going to bed.
C	Petra turn off the lights.
B	Goodnight.
A	Night.
D	JO?! JO?!
A	What's the matter?
D	JOOOO?
B	Not again. Jo's not here!
D	JO JOO!
B	Jo's not here go back to sleep.
D	I want JO JO WHERE ARE YOU? JO! JO! JO!
A	I'm quite tired. Does that happen very often?
C	You get used to it.
A	Who's Jo?
B	Not even sure he knows.
C	Petra painkillers please.
A	My mattress. It's deflated
B	It does that.
C	Sammy had terrible trouble.
D	Petra what's for breakfast?
A	My back's right on the frame.
D	Anyone know what's for breakfast?
C	You can put it on the repair list.

A	What happened to Sammy?
D	He was an idiot.
B	He took them up on it. The other option.
A	Oh.
D	JOOO JOOOO JOOOO.
A	It's cold in here.
C	Have my blanket.
D	Who used my toothbrush?
A	Petra turn the heating up.
B	It's not working.
A	Petra turn the heating up.
D	Somebody's used my toothbrush.
B	Sometimes loses connection. Oi Petra! Petra you dickhead! Turn the heating up.
D	Which one of you did it? I want to know. What am I, invisible? Somebody's used it. It's all damp. Somebody's used my toothbrush. Oi. Oi. Oi. Oi. You. Did you use it?
A	No. I.
D	Get your own toothbrush. My one's the blue one. Get your own fucking toothbrush you disgusting piece of –
A	I'd like to move please.
LIAISON	THERE'S BOUND TO BE A PERIOD OF ADJUSTMENT.
A	I was told I wouldn't be sharing with more than one person.

LIAISON   I'M AFRAID EVERYONE IS HAVING TO
SQUEEZE IN RIGHT NOW.

WE'RE TRYING TO ACCOMMODATE AS
MANY PEOPLE AS POSSIBLE.

A   I don't think I can stay here.

LIAISON   OF COURSE YOU'RE WELCOME TO LEAVE
AT ANY TIME.

A   Okay then.

LIAISON   ALTHOUGH IN YOUR CURRENT FINANCIAL
SITUATION I REALLY WOULDN'T ADVISE
IT. YOU'RE UNLIKELY TO FIND ANOTHER
RESIDENCE AT SHORT NOTICE AND THE
WEATHER'S TURNING COLD.

MAYBE YOUR SON? PERHAPS HE'D BE
HAPPY TO TAKE YOU IN?

A   He
No.

LIAISON   I'M SORRY. I REALLY NEED TO DASH.

EVERYBODY'S DOING THEIR BEST I
PROMISE YOU THAT.

HAVE YOU THOUGHT ANY MORE ABOUT
OUR EARLIER CONVERSATION?

A   I. I still need a bit more time.

B   Still here then?

A   For now.

B   Thank god. You can't leave me with these two.

D   I heard that.

C   Ah. Owwww.

A   What's the matter?

C   My back. Nerve damage.

A	I've got bad knees. Used to be a runner. The place I was in before had a physio.
B	What sort of runner?
A	Middle distance. 1500m.
D	What was it like?
A	I'm sorry?
D	The place you were in before? Have your own room?
A	Yes.
C	How lovely.
D	Oh yeah the place I'm going to's gonna have it all. My family's gonna come get me this is all just a mistake.
A	What about you?
B	Slipped in the supermarket and they made a big fuss out of nothing and took me into hospital which I couldn't afford so here I am.
C	I've got two kids.
D	Nobody asked.
C	Have you any?
A	A son.
B	She already told you that don't you listen?
C	And you'd do anything for him I bet?
A	Yeah. I would.
D	This is boring.
C	My girl she's got a boy of her own.
D	Really boring.
C	He looks like me you know you can see it. So when they offered it I was always gonna say yes.

A   You said yes?

B   Didn't you know?
             Not with us long are you mate?

C   Three weeks I've got.

A   I'm sorry.

C   Don't be!
             Show me where to sign I said.
             The compensation. It's a lot of money.

B   Not enough.

C   My kids are having a tough time.
             They'd have taken me in but I couldn't ask them.
             They can't afford that.
             So I said
             Let me help. Let me do this for you.
             Didn't know them much when they were little so.
             Right thing to do.
             S'what they say.

B   Who?

C   Um. Globally speaking.
             What with the climate and
             Economy. All that.

             Taking up space.

             My kids didn't fight me on it.

             One of them even drove me here.

             Don't come and visit me I said.
             And they haven't.

             Good kids. Respect my wishes.

A   Can't believe it.

B   He's a fool.

A   You think so?

B	You don't? You're not thinking of doing it?
A	Don't know. Maybe.
B	You mad? Come on. This place isn't perfect but
A	They say it's painless.
B	Who's gonna contradict them? Shuts down your nervous system. Sounds pretty painful to me.
A	You don't think it's brave?
B	Brave? Stupid.
A	But if it helps
B	Helps who? You haven't got a responsibility to them. They've got a responsibility to you. That's the way it's supposed to be.
A	I'm not sure that
B	Whole country's acting like it's some big surprise that there's suddenly so many of us. Like we all just fell out the sky. Like it just started raining old people. They knew this mess was coming. They knew for years and they looked the other way. They want you to make it easy on them. Don't give them the satisfaction. There is plenty of life to be had, even in a place like this.
A	Okay. I've made up my mind. It's a no. No thank you.
LIAISON	OF COURSE. THAT'S ABSOLUTELY FINE. I'LL MAKE A NOTE. YOU CAN ALWAYS CHANGE YOUR MIND IF YOU WANT.

A   I don't think I will.

LIAISON   BY THE WAY. YOUR SON. WE'VE
                  MANAGED TO TRACK HIM DOWN.

B   How fast did you used to run then?

A   Pretty fast. Ran for my county. Coulda gone
                  national.

                  Do you know. I can't remember what it feels like.
                  Being able to do that. I've tried and tried. But
                  I can't remember.

B   Your bed still broke?

A   Yes.

B   Mine's pretty comfortable.

A   Good for you.

B   What I'm saying is. If yours is broken. You can
                  always share with me.

                  If you like.

A   Oh.

B   Morning.

A   Last night.

B   Was nice.

A   It's been a while.

B   No kidding.

A   I didn't know if

B   It's okay.

                  You're just about the only thing that makes it
                  bearable in here.
                  Do you know that?

                  So.

                  Wanna do it again?

D   JOOO. JOOOOO. JOOOO.

C   Ah! Ah!

B   Not you too.

A   What's the matter?

C   It hurts.

B   It's alright.

C   My back. My legs.
           Please. Ohhh. Please.
           Petra painkillers.

D   What's going on?

C   Painkillers please!

D   Too much noise.

A   Help him.

C   Aaaah.

B   Petra's not working.

A   Where are they?

B   Connection's down.

C   Petra painkillers. Help me. Help. Ah.

B   They'll fix it tomorrow.

D   Too much noise it's late.

A   He can't wait that long.

C   Ahhhh it hurts. It hurts. Ah ah ah. Painkillers.

B   I know. Shh. It's okay.

A   Shouldn't we call someone?

B   We can't.

D   This is why I'm getting outta here.

B   Shut up will you

D   Get my own nurse. A proper person.

B   Shut up!

C   Oh god please!

D   Tell me to shut up? Tell him!

C   Petra!

A   It's not working mate I'm sorry.

C   Ah ah ah Jesus!

D   When my nephew realises.

C   Ohhhh
Ohhhhh. Ah. Ohhhh.

D   He's shit himself.

C   Oh Jesus I'm sorry I'm

B   It's alright hey. We'll get you all cleaned up.

Don't worry.

C   I want. I want it over. Please.

B   I know. I know you do.

Try and get some rest.

C   Aaaaaah.
Ohhhhh.
Aaaaaah.
No. N. No.
Aaaaaah.
Aaaaaah.
Petra please.
Ohhhhh.
Aaaaaah.

A   All night.

They can't just leave him like that.
It's still not back online.
We should say something.
Make a complaint.

D	Oi. You two. I saw you.
B	Did ya?
D	I saw you both together.
B	That's nice.
D	It's disgusting. I'm disgusted.
A	What did you see?
D	You should know better. You're too old. It's not.
B	What?
D	Hygienic.
B	You a bit jealous?
D	I'm gonna tell.
B	Tell who?
D	Then you'll be sorry.
A	I still think we should say something. They can't leave us offline for this long.
B	Your bed been fixed yet?
LIAISON	IT'S BEEN BROUGHT TO OUR ATTENTION THAT YOU'RE SHARING A BED.
A	By who?
LIAISON	I'M AFRAID THAT ISN'T ALLOWED.
A	Why not?
LIAISON	IT'S NOT HYGIENIC. YOU HAVE YOUR OWN BED
A	So?
LIAISON	SO WHY WOULD YOU WANT TO SHARE WITH SOMEONE ELSE?
A	My mattress deflated. My back was sore.

LIAISON   I'LL MAKE SURE THAT'S PUT ON THE
            REPAIR SCHEDULE. WE'LL GET IT FIXED
            RIGHT AWAY.

A   You've been saying that for weeks.

LIAISON   BUT NO MORE BED SHARING EH? IF IT
            HAPPENS AGAIN I'LL HAVE TO GIVE YOU
            A WARNING.

            LOOK. IF IT WERE UP TO ME

A   Isn't it?

LIAISON   THINGS WOULD BE VERY DIFFERENT IF
            IT WERE.

            I'M SORRY. I REALLY AM.

            BUT YOU SIGNED AN AGREEMENT
            STATING YOU'D FOLLOW THE FACILITY
            RULES. RESIDENTS WHO REPEATEDLY
            BREAK THEM CAN BE EJECTED.

            COME ON. YOU DON'T WANT TO FIND
            YOURSELF OUT ON THE STREET, DO YOU?

C   So. My last afternoon.

D   Good.

A   How are you feeling?

C   Good. Great.
            Yes.
            Funny knowing. Like Christmas Eve.

D   Not really.

C   My kids sent a message. Thoughtful.
            I thought we could have a bit of a send-off.
            I asked Petra for some cake.

B   You're joking.

C   Nothing special. Something to mark the occasion.

B   The occasion?

D	What sort of cake?
C	Have a nice time before I
D	Looks disgusting.
A	Go on then.

C *passes round cake. Everyone eats cake.*
A moment.

C *sings their favourite song. They sort of forget the*
words a bit and A *helps them.* D *doesn't join in.*

C   I told them.
Don't visit me.

Like pruning the trees in the garden.
Room for new growth.

My life's just been shredded paper.
Deleted emails.

My kids.
That's what's important.
Their kids.
Don't come and visit me I said.
We kept my dad alive till he was ninety-three.
Couldn't remember his own name.

God.

Bit nervous actually.

My leg. Let me just.

What will it be like do you think? After?

A   I don't know.

C   Do you believe in God?

B   No.

C   I do.
I mean.
I try to anyway.

Listen to me.
Going on a bit aren't I?

D   Yes.

C   Petra, what time is it?

In a way we're lucky aren't we?
To get this far.

C *tells a story about a time they did something*
physically impressive when they were young.
The story starts:

One time, when I was about ____ years old I

_____

That was nice.

I better go.

They're waiting for me.

Don't want to be late.

Just.

Let me just sit here for a minute.

A   Do you think it went alright?

D   Who's gonna take his bed?

A   Where should we go?

B   Bathroom.

A   They caught us last time.

B   Outside?

A   Quiet!

B   Bedroom's empty.

A   That was.

B   I know.

A   Bathroom again?

B	Quiet.
A	Is he asleep?
B	Think so.
D	I'm not asleep.
B	Oh oh
D	I can hear everything.
A	Happy birthday.
B	Come here.
A	It's getting cold. I feel
B	Petra play 'All I Want For Christmas Is You'.
A	Petra please stop!
B	Dance with me.
D	What are you doing?
A	Happy new year.
B	You look
A	Shut up. So do you.
B	Morning.
A	Morning.
B	Morning.
A	Morning.
B	First album?
A	Petra play [*artist name*]
	B *reacts to this choice*.
	Let's get out of here. Me and you.
B	Yeah? Where will we go?
A	Brazil. We'll sit on the beach nude.
B	Nobody wants to see that.

A   I do.

B   We'll make everyone retch.

A   I'll rip the sink from the wall and hurl it through
           the window and we can make a break for it.

           They kiss.

           I

           I

           Oh.

           I love you. Shit. I never thought I'd say that again.

D   What are you both doing?

           Don't think I don't know what you're doing.

           People like you it's disgusting you're disgusting.

           Shouldn't have to be in here with people like you
           this was never meant to happen never meant to
           happen to me people in my family live a long time
           you know good genes my dad he lived for a long
           time and my brother is still healthy his son lives in
           America he's the one that's going to pay for me to
           transfer out of here I need my own space you see
           need my sleep don't want to share with the likes of
           you where I'm going they got everything you need
           and they know how to treat someone our age fuck
           this place you know this place is shit fuck them
           putting me in this place like I'm no one I'm only
           in here because of a mistake it's not right I got
           somewhere got somewhere to go I'm gonna talk to
           them tomorrow and

           and

           No.

           Try him again.

           Try him again please.

           No no no no.

A	What's wrong?
D	No no no no no no
B	They got through to his nephew.
D	No no no no no
A	There actually is a nephew?
B	Said he can't help.
D	No I can't I'm not sposed to Jo Jo JO JO
B	It's alright.
D	I WON'T.
B	Calm down.
D	I WON'T TAKE IT I DON'T WANT TO
A	What happened?
D	I'LL SPIT IT OUT.
B	He said yes. After they told him the nephew weren't coming he signed, stupid bastard. Don't think he knew what he was signing.
D	I didn't didn't know. They tricked me tricked me.
A	When?
B	Tomorrow.
D	I WON'T DO IT I WON'T PLEASE.
A	That seems fast.
D	PLEASE PLEASE.
A	Surely there's something
B	Not once he's signed. I'm sorry mate, that's it.
D	No no no it's not right it's a mistake.
B	You understand what's going on?

D   My nephew's gonna come he's gonna come and
        get me.

B   He said no, love.

D   Please I don't want to.

B   Why did you sign it?
        Why did you let them?

A   It's not right.

D   I don't know.
        I don't want to.
        My family live for a long time.

        Please.

        My nephew try him again will you?

B   It's not up to me. I wish it was.

D   No.
        I don't want to.
        Not yet. Not yet. Not yet.

        Try him again will you?

A   They didn't have to be so rough.

B   Wouldn't calm down.

A   Why didn't the nephew come?

B   The way things are right now?
        People can barely take care of themselves. It's not
        like he was the easiest person in the world.

        My niece is coming.

A   That's nice.

B   That's odd.

A   I'd like to meet her.
        I don't understand.
        You're leaving?

B   She's come into some money.
        Offered to take me in.

A   Oh.
           That's.
           Say no.

B   I can't.

A   You can tell them you want to stay want to

B   You know it doesn't work like that.
           I've got somewhere I can go. So I'm going.

           I'll come visit.

A   It's so far away.

B   Maybe you could get transferred

           I don't know what you want me to say.

           It might be nice.
           Be around family.
           Her kids are a bit much.
           But it might be nice.

A   Okay. Then. Well.

           You should pack.

B   Don't be angry with me.

A   I'm not.

B   It's not my fault.

           Please.

           I want to say goodbye.

           Okay then.

           I'll see you.

A   Bye.

           Where is she?

LIAISON   CALM DOWN.

A   I want to talk to her I want you to tell me how to
           contact her.

LIAISON   I DON'T HAVE THAT INFORMATION I'M
           SORRY.

A   She hasn't been online since she left.

LIAISON   I'M SURE IT'S JUST TAKEN A WHILE FOR
           HER TO ADJUST TO HER NEW
           SURROUNDINGS.

A   It's been weeks she hasn't messaged me and I don't
           know what's happened to her I don't know how she
           is or

LIAISON   I'M SURE SHE'S FINE. LOOK, I'LL DO MY
           BEST TO CHECK ON HER.

           LISTEN. YOU SHOULD BE HAPPY FOR HER.
           HER FAMILY SEEMED LIKE VERY NICE
           PEOPLE. SHE'S GOING TO BE VERY
           COMFORTABLE. I'M SURE SHE'LL GET IN
           CONTACT WHEN SHE'S READY.

           AND I'VE GOT SOME GOOD NEWS FOR
           YOU. A SINGLE UNIT'S JUST COME
           AVAILABLE.

A   What?

LIAISON   I MADE SURE TO PUT YOUR NAME
           FORWARD. A ROOM TO YOURSELF.

BELIEVE ME. IT DOESN'T HAPPEN VERY OFTEN.

THAT'LL BE NICE WON'T IT. BIT OF SPACE?

A is all alone.

A   Petra I'm home.

Petra turn on the lights.

She moves. She moves back. A day goes by.

Petra turn off the lights.

Petra turn on the lights.

She moves. She moves back. A day goes by.

Petra turn off the lights.

Petra turn on the lights.

She moves. She moves back. A week goes by.

Petra turn off the lights.

Petra turn on the lights.

She moves. She moves back. A month goes by.

Petra turn off the lights.

Petra turn on the lights.

She moves. She moves back. Two months go by.

Petra turn off the lights.

Petra turn on the lights.

She moves. She moves back. Three months go by.

Petra turn off the lights.

Petra turn on the lights.
Petra turn off the lights.
Petra turn on the lights.
Petra turn off the lights.
Petra turn on the lights.

Petra

I want an appointment.

LIAISON	ARE YOU SURE ABOUT THIS?
A	Yes. I'm sure. I'll do it.
	My son.
	His family. They'll definitely get the money?
LIAISON	OF COURSE. THE FULL COMPENSATION.
	WOULD YOU LIKE TO SPEAK TO HIM? WE HAVE A CONTACT NUMBER.
A	No. That's okay.
LIAISON	WE DO STRONGLY ADVISE THAT YOU CONSULT WITH YOUR FAMILY BEFORE COMMITTING TO THIS COURSE OF ACTION.
	DON'T YOU WANT TO TALK IT THROUGH WITH HIM? OR SOMEONE ELSE?
A	No.
LIAISON	OKAY.
A	What's the next step?
LIAISON	WELL. I'LL HAVE YOU LOOK OVER SOME DOCUMENTS TO SIGN. WE'LL REQUEST ACCESS TO YOUR WILL. DO YOU HAVE ANY LIFE INSURANCE POLICIES THAT WE SHOULD
A	No.
	How long will I have to wait?
LIAISON	HAVING A LOOK, THE EARLIEST WE CAN SCHEDULE YOU IN FOR IS... OH, TUESDAY.

A   That soon?

LIAISON   WE CAN AIM FOR LATER IF YOU LIKE.
           I CAN GIVE YOU A LIST OF DATES.

           EVERYBODY'S DIFFERENT. SOME PEOPLE
           LIKE TO GET IT OUT OF THE WAY ONCE
           THEY'VE MADE THE DECISION. OTHERS
           LIKE TO SPEND A FEW WEEKS OR MONTHS

A   Yes. I. I think Tuesday might be best.

LIAISON   CAN I JUST SAY. YOU'RE MAKING A VERY
           BRAVE DECISION.

           I'M SURE YOUR SON AND HIS FAMILY
           WILL COME TO APPRECIATE IT.

A   Thank you for all your help.

           I know you've been. Trying.

LIAISON   THANK YOU. THAT MEANS A LOT.

           I WISH I COULD'VE DONE MORE.

A   Will I. Will I be alone?

           A alone. Sits for a while.

           A NURSE *enters. Smiles.*

NURSE   Are you comfortable enough?

A   Yes. Thank you. Is it time already?

NURSE   Almost. Have you got everything you need?

A   Yes.

NURSE   Enough pillows? Is the mattress okay?

           The NURSE *puts down two cups of liquid.*

A   What's in them?

NURSE   The drugs?

A   Yes.

NURSE	Didn't they tell you?
A	No.
NURSE	Oh. The first one is an antiemetic. That means it stops nausea and vomiting. Stops you feeling sick. I'm going to need you to take this one first.
	She takes it.
	That's it. Well done.
A	And this one?
NURSE	Well. That is fifteen grams of powdered pentobutanol dissolved in water.
A	Powdered pentobutanol. That's fun to say. Powdered pentobutanol.
NURSE	Do you know what it does?
A	Yes.
	Will it hurt?
NURSE	No.
A	I don't mind if it does. So long as it doesn't take long. Will it take long?
NURSE	No. You'll get a bit thirsty. And then drowsy. And then. It will be just like going to sleep. There is absolutely nothing to be afraid of. I promise.
A	Have you done a lot of these?
NURSE	I have.
A	And what's that like?
NURSE	Well. I think it's one of the most important jobs there is.
A	My son. This will help him.
NURSE	Do you need some more time?

A   No.

NURSE   Because I won't rush you. It's my job to make you
           as comfortable as possible.

A   Will you be here?

NURSE   I can leave the room if you want. Or I can stay.
           It's up to you.

A   Stay. Please.

NURSE   I'll be right here the whole time.

A   How old are you?

NURSE   I'm twenty-three.

A   Oh. Just a baby.

           Do you have children?

NURSE   No.

A   A boyfriend? Girlfriend?

NURSE   No.

           Do you need some more time?

A   No. No. I'm fine.

NURSE   Are you comfortable enough?

A   I just drink it straight down?

NURSE   Straight down.

           It's okay. I'm here. I'm here with you.

A   Okay. Just. Okay.

NURSE   Are there any words you'd like to say?

A   Cheers.

           She drinks it.

           Oh!

I remember!

It feels like

Flying I'm flying round the bend on the last lap
my long legs barely even touching the floor
another girl coming up on my shoulder and now
shit they're ahead of me keep calm there's enough
time left I can catch her I've got the stride I've got
such a long stride work those legs focus on
breathing focus on stride that's it clicking now I'm
catching her we're almost side by side I'm going
to do this I'm going to win dig deep find
something extra almost there

Everything in my wonderful body is singing

Run don't fall keep running don't fall I am so fast
I am so fast it's almost over the finish is almost
here it's coming too quick there's not enough time
there's not enough time there's not enough time

and I dip for the line and

www.nickhernbooks.co.uk

facebook.com/nickhernbooks

twitter.com/nickhernbooks